W0187570

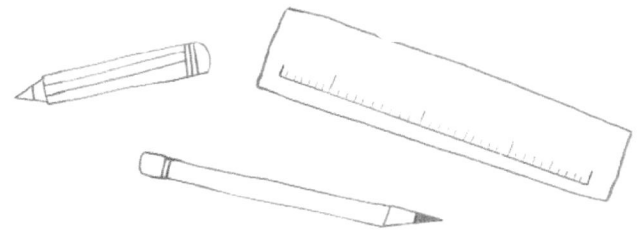

THANK YOU, TEACHER

Written by Rachel Elliot

First published in Great Britain in 2025 by Wren & Rook

Text copyright © Hodder & Stoughton 2025
Illustrations copyright © Catherine Booth 2025
All rights reserved.

ISBN: 978 1 5263 6752 5

SRD

MIX
Paper | Supporting
responsible forestry
FSC **FSC™ C104740**
www.fsc.org

Wren & Rook
An imprint of
Hachette Children's Group
Part of Hodder & Stoughton Limited
Carmelite House
50 Victoria Embankment
London EC4Y 0DZ

The authorised representative in the EEA is Hachette Ireland, 8 Castlecourt Centre,
Castleknock Road, Castleknock, Dublin 15, D15 XTP3, Ireland
(email: info@hbgi.ie).

An Hachette UK Company
www.hachette.co.uk
www.hachettechildrens.co.uk

Printed and bound in India by Manipal Technologies Limited, Manipal

THANK YOU, TEACHER

wren
&rook

This book was written by

....

THANK YOU

6

Dear ....,

My time in .... class
has been **unforgettable**.

The **funniest** moment was when

....

....

My **favourite** trip was

....

....

The lesson I **enjoyed** most was

....

....

My biggest **success** was

....

....

Thank you for teaching me

that every day is a brand-new start,

like a fresh sheet of paper.

Old mistakes are in the past,

and I can let them go.

The **future** is not written yet.

I am looking forward

to today's adventures.

Thank you for teaching me
to listen carefully. That's how
I find out about the world.

It's a **superpower** to say,
'I don't know'.
Those words help me to
understand new ideas.

Thank you for teaching me

to love myself just the way I am.

I am happy to be me.

No one can make me feel small

when I **believe** in myself.

Draw yourself here

13

Thank you for teaching me

to use kindness as a tool.

I have learned that it can make

the world a better place.

I am kind to myself because

I deserve to be **happy**.

Being kind is always

the best choice.

16

Thank you for teaching me

to think before I speak.

First, I ask myself three questions:

Is it **true**?

Is it **kind**?

Is it **necessary**?

The way I treat other people

shows everyone what

sort of person I am.

Thank you for teaching me

that respect and trust are

like building blocks.

They create strong friendships.

When I am polite to other people,

it helps me to **respect** myself.

Being respected is more important

than being popular.

Thank you for teaching me

to always tell the truth,

no matter how hard that is.

Holding on to the **truth** is like

sailing a boat through a storm.

I can trust it to guide me

safely to the other side.

Thank you for teaching me

that being fair is a choice

I can make every day.

I have learned that I can

make a difference in the world

just by being **honest**.

Thank you for teaching me

that my ideas matter.

I am always **free**

to change my mind.

Thank you for teaching me
to be true to myself.

I know the difference
between right and wrong,
and I can stand up
for my **beliefs**.

Stick a photo of yourself

playing games here

Thank you for teaching me
that learning can be fun.

I learn when I am playing
games and being silly, and there
is **always time** for a joke.

Thank you for teaching me
to be patient. The best things
are worth waiting for.

Like a leaf floating in a stream,
sometimes I must **wait and see**
where the water takes me.

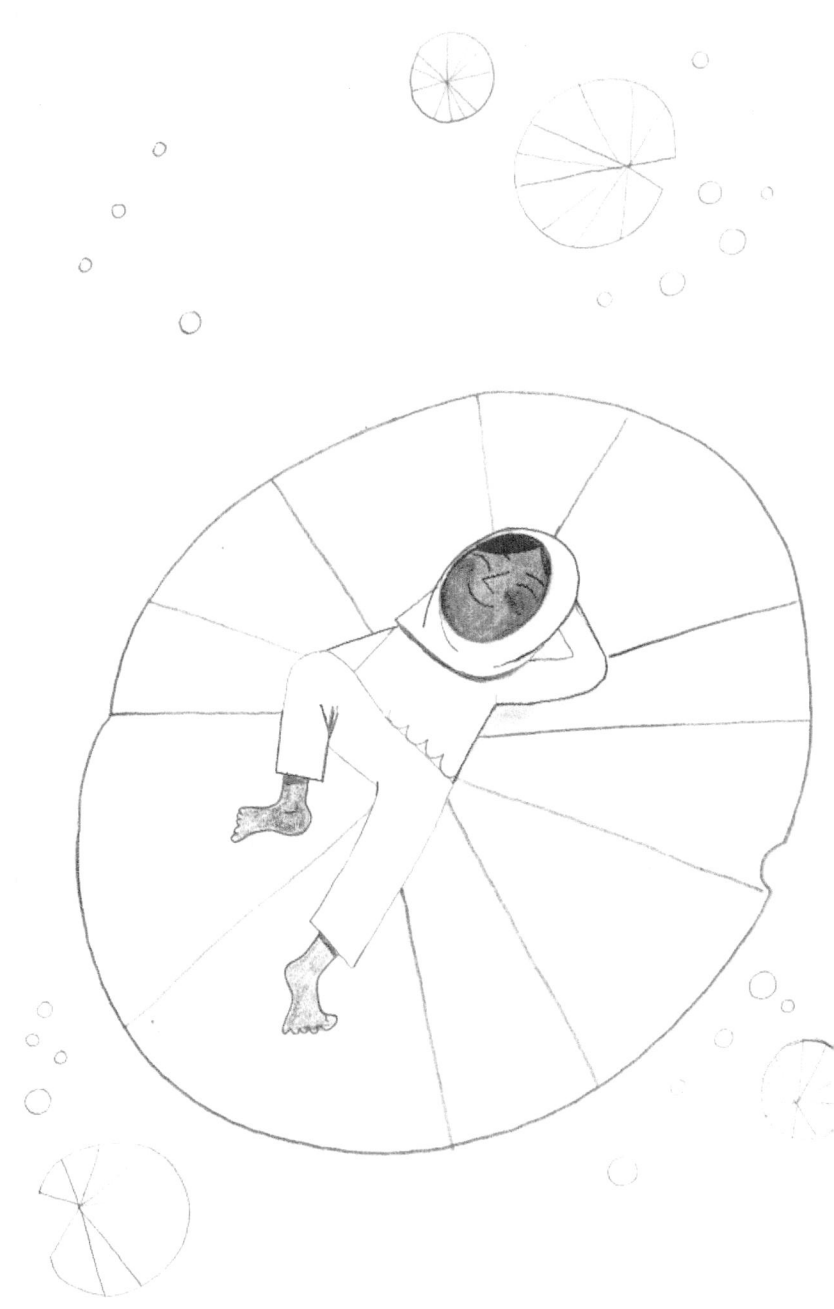

Thank you for teaching me
to be understanding.
Everyone's worries are big to them,
even if they seem small to me.

Other people have fears and
worries too. **Understanding** them
helps me to be a better friend.

Thank you for teaching me
to forgive myself. My mistakes
show me how to get things right.

THANK

There is no such thing as **perfect**.

Thank you for teaching me

that it is brave to ask for help.

Courage comes in all

shapes and sizes.

Sometimes it is loud and proud.

Sometimes it is as quiet as a mouse.

Thank you for teaching me

that my emotions are

never wrong. It is OK to show

my big feelings and let them flow.

My thoughts have power over
my feelings. When I expect something
to be scary, I feel afraid.
When I expect it to be easy,
I feel calm.

Thank you for teaching me
to talk about my worries.
Most problems feel smaller
when I share them.

I can enjoy the **happy times**
while they are happening
and remember that difficult times
won't last forever.

40

41

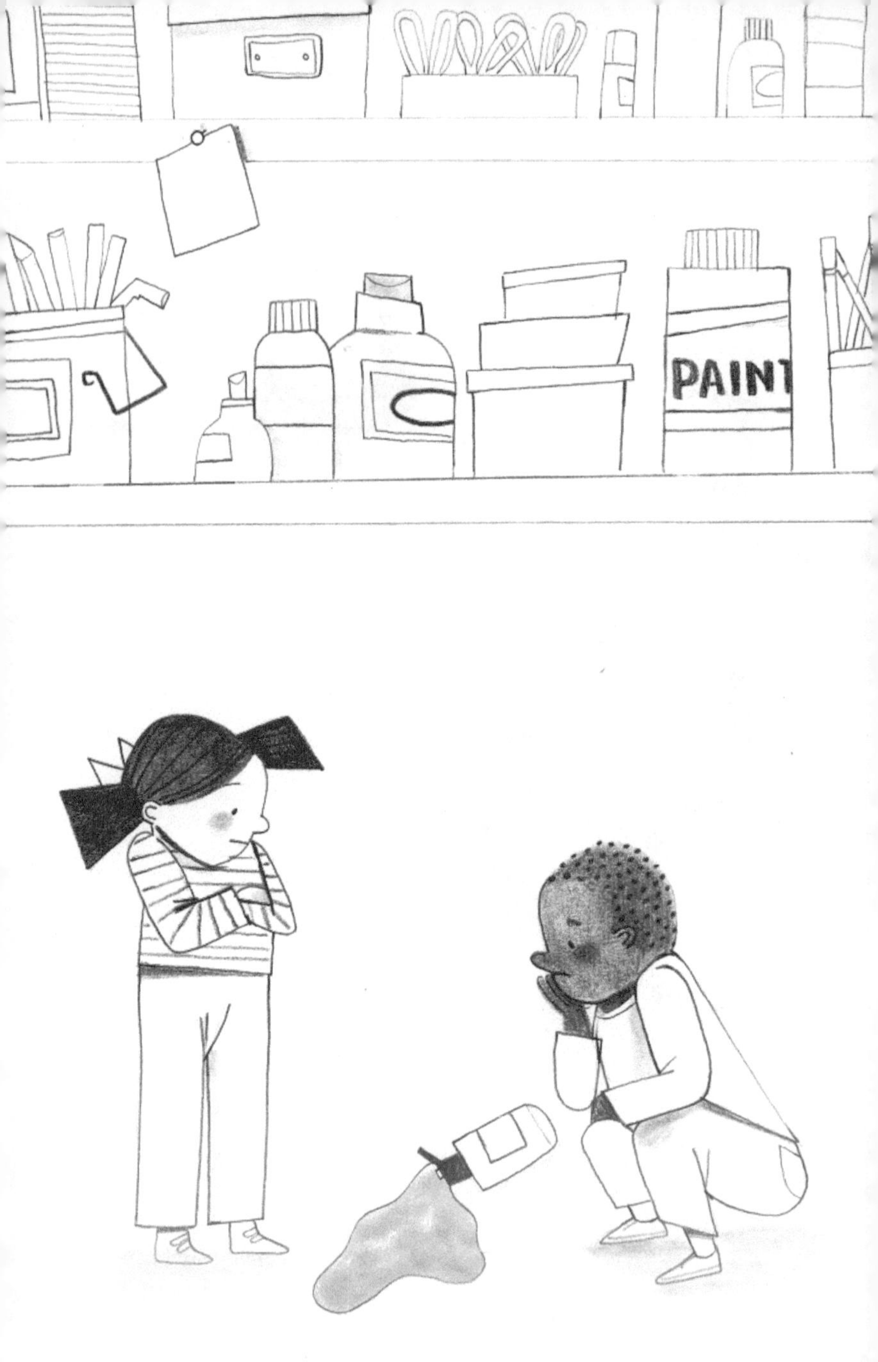
PAINT

Thank you for teaching me

to pause and breathe when

things seem tough. I can count

to ten before I react.

I have **control** over how

I choose to behave.

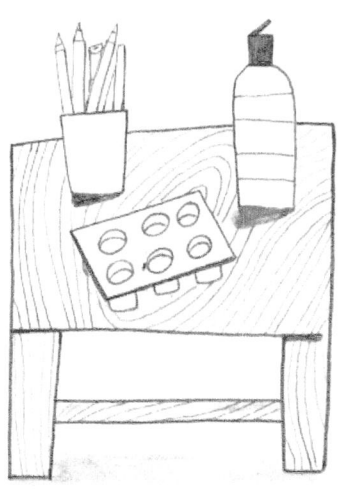

Thank you for teaching me

to use my imagination. My life

is a picture that I am painting.

I add new **colours** to it every day.

It is important to choose colours I like.

Draw a picture of your teacher here

45

Thank you for teaching me
to always try my best.
I can keep going, even when
things seem hard.

Being first doesn't always mean
being the best. Some people come
last because they stop
to **help** others.

Thank you for showing me
that I can choose who I
spend time with. I make friends
who are **kind, honest and confident**.

I accept other people for who
they are. They are the best at
being them, and I am the
best at being me.

BEST

AT
BEING ME

Thank you for teaching me

to be excited about change.

All living things **change and grow** with

the sun and the rain to feed them.

You have **shone** your light on

the best parts of my character.

Your lessons will help me **grow**

into the best me I can be.

ME and YOU!

Stick a photo of you and your teacher here

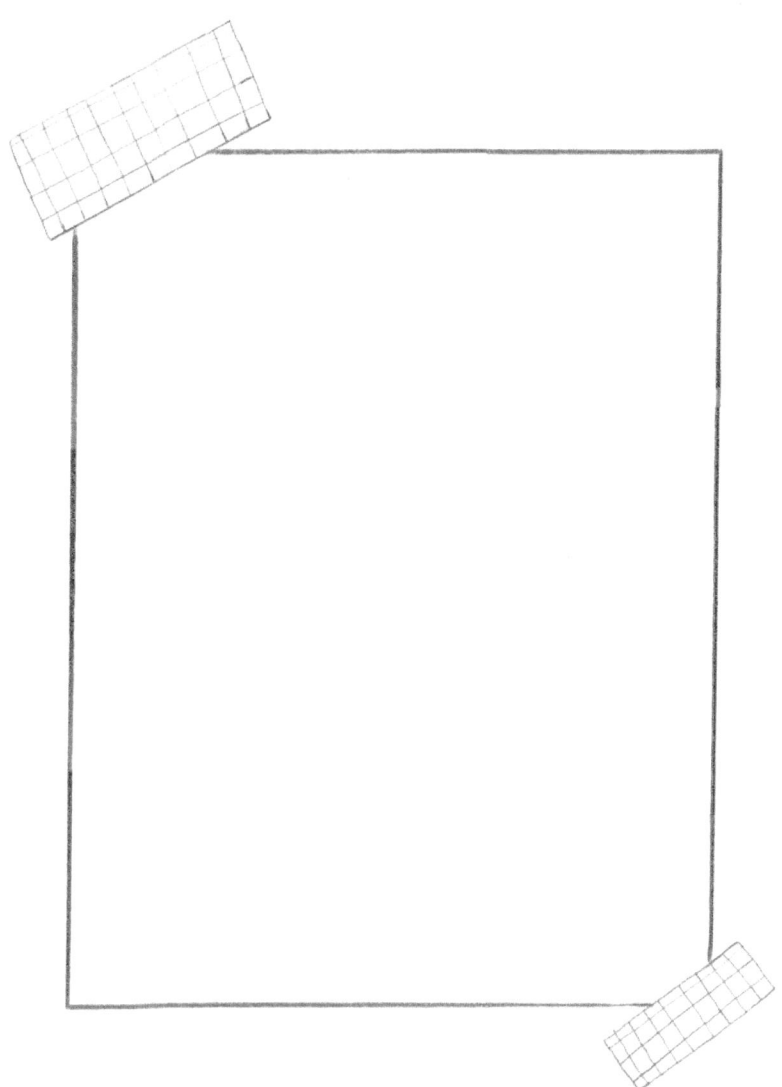

I am so **glad** you are my teacher because

....

....

....

....

You have **always** made me feel

....

....

With you as my teacher, I have **discovered**

....

....

....

The things I will **never forget**

about being in your class are:

....

....

....

....

Most of all, **thank you** for

all you have taught me.

Every classroom should have

a teacher as ....

and .... as you.

Love from ....

HELP YOUR STUDENTS SHINE WITH

by Rosie Jones

Beat the Bullies, Make Fearless Friends

and Deal with Funny Fails

THESE CONFIDENCE-BOOSTING BOOKS:

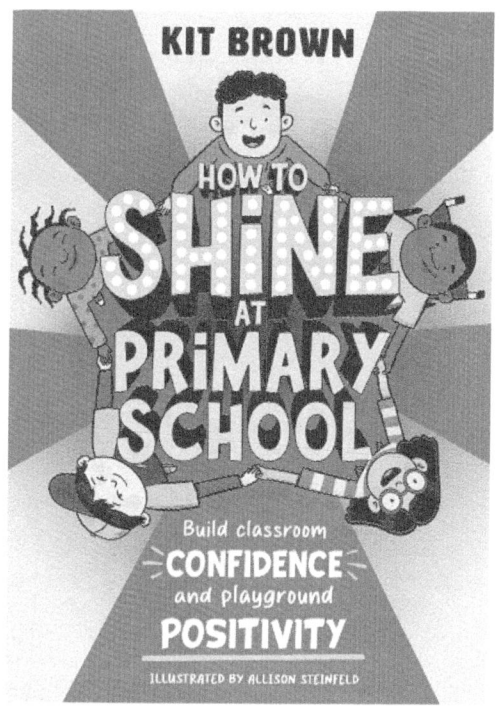

by Kit Brown

Build Class Room Confidence

and Playground Positivity